INNOCENT BADGER V[...]

Published in Great Britain by Innocent Badger Books
© Innocent Badger Books 2015   ISBN 9 780993 474309

INTRODUCTION

Firstly I must thank all the people who helped to make this book a reality - friends, sab groups, the patrol groups of the badger cull zones, all the people who backed the project and, of course, you for purchasing it.

I first started campaigning against the badger cull in June 2012 Like so many people I have met, I didn't believe then (and I still find it hard to understand now) that a badger cull could ever be a possibility. Three years on and the unnecessary slaughter is very much a reality.

In that time, we as a movement have gone from very humble beginnings and grown in leaps and bounds to become probably the largest "direct action" animal rights campaign ever. The scale of the protests now involves thousands of people who, whether doing an hour a day or the full six weeks, make the culling of badgers an impossible task for the cattle farming industry.

We have seen Owen "Patsy" Paterson MP, the man behind the culls, arrive and depart. He promised the farming community two culls in 2012 followed by a rollout each year to a further ten zones. As I write this in late 2015, we currently have to deal with three cull zones - nowhere near the 32 that Patsy envisaged.

Our success has surprised me as much as anyone. I remember going to my first public meeting in Taunton in those early days. Brian May and the heads of several animal charities spoke at length about the science and morality of the culls, but none of them touched upon what any of us could do about it beyond signing the petition and writing to our MPs.

I'd gone with a few other activists and, during the Q&A, I outlined the "Stop the Cull" plan. We needed 70 people to sign up to do patrols in each area. Each person would be asked to commit to six nights each, equating to ten people out in each zone every night.

I would often candidly admit to other activists that I didn't think we had a hope in hell of ever getting more than a handful of people out in total and even if we did manage to get the mythical 70 people, how could we possibly be effective in an area that was hundreds of square miles?

The press informed the UK not only about Brian May's petition, but also a growing army of committed activists preparing to go out night after night to disrupt the culling. It soon became apparent that journalists were hungry for any activist-related stories so we fed them an endless stream of campaign updates; the more controversial, the more they lapped it up.

All of the press coverage, combined with a relentless social media campaign, would reveal to even a casual observer that our initial recruitment goals had been achieved ten times over. The police were so worried that due to the resource-hungry summer Olympics, they were blatantly undermanned so the 2012 badger cull was cancelled.

2013 saw hunt saboteur groups from across the country pledge to help when the culls started and many travelled huge distances week after week to help map out all the badger setts. On the very first night of the cull in the Somerset cull zone, Bristol Hunt Sabs, armed with one of the five £80 "Aldi" night vision monoculars we possessed, found the glow of the shooters' infrared lamps. The moment that the killers realised they'd been spotted, they packed up and ran away – a pattern which has continued to this day.

Crowdfunding via our now infamous Facebook pages (the controversy paid off) soon equipped us with top of the range night vision equipment. That kit, combined with detailed sett maps and a rapid communication network constantly relaying the location of shooters' vehicles across the zones, had us finding the killers night after night and stopping them repeatedly.

The first year's target number to be killed totalled a minimum of 5,000 badgers. The killers failed by a huge margin and instead of admitting that they could never reach the required amount, they did what they did best - told lies. The government & the NFU, after spending the last year and half telling the country there was a badger "population explosion", now decided that actually there weren't very many badgers at all and that was the reason they couldn't kill enough. Mr Paterson's career-ending quote - "the badgers moved the goalposts" - still makes me smile.

When you add up all the weeks of culling in all the zones over the last three years; 21 in Somerset, 24 in Gloucestershire and 6 in the newly-added Dorset, the total after the 2015 cull is 51 bloody weeks and yet after all those weeks of slaughter, yes thousands of badgers have been killed, but they still are nowhere near the target of 5,000 that they wanted to kill in the first year.

Direct action alone is responsible for the failure of these culls and, being the spokesperson for the group, much of its success is wrongly attributed to me. Along with misdirected praise comes misdirected anger. Being smeared in the press doesn't particularly bother me - it is a bit disconcerting for a few days but life goes on.

The National Farmers' Union went further than just the usual name-calling and took out an injunction to try to stop me and everyone else involved in protests. Of the £200,000 that they've spent so far on this dubious legal route, they are trying to recoup £120,000 of it from me via court costs.

Unfortunately I don't have that sort of money spare to give them, so they might have to wait a while. To keep the farmers happy, I have planned to write a series of vegan cookbooks in the hope that one may one day sell well enough to pay them off.

This first cookbook has taken me a lot longer than expected to compile. Many recipes were sent in by friends and groups, I rewrote many of them so that the writing style was consistent, then after some thought I decided that the book would be far more authentic if the original authors' voices were kept.

I'd planned to include some nutrition guidelines in the book but, after extensive online research, I feel it is important that everyone does their own research or asks the Vegan Society for an information pack. The most important advice that I can give anyone is that you have a varied healthy diet. Yes, quinoa is a superfood, as are buckwheat and hemp seeds, but you don't have to live on them, nor should you eat peanut butter on brown bread every day and think you're eating healthily! Variety is essential.

The one vitamin that is often of concern to vegans is B12. Interestingly, B12 can be found as bacteria growing on unwashed plants pulled from the ground. If you don't eat several portions of raw plants complete with soil every day, you really should take a B12 supplement. Don't just rely on cereals and plant milks fortified with it - an individual's absorption of B12 and the actual availability of it in the food can vary from person to person, day to day and meal to meal.

I went vegan in 1997 and didn't take any supplements until 2012. I'd started getting really tired in the afternoon; this may have been due to me having not eaten properly for a few months. To rectify the tiredness as quickly as possible, I packed up my pasta for dinner and ditched the toast for breakfast and lunch. For breakfast, I went over to muesli (high in nuts and seeds) topped with fresh fruit. Lunch now always involves leafy greens and I don't have pasta for dinner more than twice a week, even though it is my favourite!

I also started taking the "Veg1" supplement, which the Vegan Society sells. A 6-month supply of 180 tablets costs less than £12, which works out at under a penny a day. The afternoon naps I'd required came to an end within a week.

I hope that whether you are new to veganism or not, you enjoy the recipes in this book and I hope you'll look out for my next cookbook, which I aim to have ready for spring/summer 2016.

For the badgers.

Gamal "Jay" Tiernan

THICK POTATO AND COCONUT SOUP

1 LARGE POTATO OR TWO MEDIUM ONES
2 BIG ONIONS (MORE ONION THAN POTATO)
1 TIN COCONUT MILK
1 HOT CHILLI
1 PINCH ASAFOETIDA (OPTIONAL)
20 CURRY LEAVES (OPTIONAL)

Peel the potato and onions.

Chop the potato into medium dice and the onion into very thin slices.

Combine with all the ingredients in a big pan and add two tins worth of water.

Boil for about half an hour until it's all cooked through.

Stir well every so often to make sure it doesn't stick. It should dry out a bit so don't have a lid on it for at least the last ten minutes.

RED LENTIL SOUP

1/2 LB RED LENTILS (WASHED)
HALF A HEAD OF FINELY CHOPPED CELERY
3 CHOPPED CARROTS
1 LARGE CHOPPED ONION
A LOT OF CHOPPED GARLIC
2 LARGE BAY LEAVES
CUMIN SEEDS TO TASTE (1 OR 2 TSP)
OIL FOR FRYING
SALT
HALF A LEMON OR SOME DRIED CHILLI FLAKES FOR AN ADDED KICK

1. In a saucepan, lightly toast 1 or 2 tsp of whole cumin seed jus
   until they start to give off their scent- be careful not to brow
   them.

2. Add olive or sunflower oil and all the chopped veg, bay leave
   (whole, but crush them a bit in your hand before adding) an
   garlic.

3. Cover the pan and sweat the veg until they're all tender. Keep a
   much moisture inside the pan as possible, but stir regularly – thi
   will take about 15mins on a low heat – add some black pepper t
   taste (don't add any salt until the end as this will inhibit the uptak
   of water for the lentils).

4. Add the lentils and coat in the mixture before adding twice a
   much water as lentils (cup for cup is best), add half a lemon, cove
   and simmer very gently – the lentils don't need to boil hard t
   cook, expand and dissolve, which they should do after half a
   hour.

5. Add salt to taste and the soup is now ready to eat, but I prefer t
   let it cool and really thicken up (I have been known to rename i
   pate at this stage and eat it on toast) before loosening with wate
   and reheating.

OLLA GITANA

THIS IS A BIG HEARTY SPANISH SOUP RECIPE. USE A LARGE PAN OR SMALLER AMOUNTS OF VEG/CHICKPEAS.

3 PINTS VEGETABLE STOCK
1LB CHICK PEAS (COOKED WEIGHT)
1 LARGE FAT CARROT, DICED
1LB PUMPKIN/SQUASH, CUT INTO CHUNKS
10OZ RUNNER BEANS, SLICED INTO 1" PIECES
2 FIRM PEARS, CORED & CUT INTO EIGHTHS
1 TBS OLIVE OIL
3 CLOVES GARLIC, MINCED
4 OZ GROUND ALMONDS
2TSP SHERRY VINEGAR (IS TRADITIONAL IN THIS RECIPE, BUT RED WINE VINEGAR WILL DO)
1 LARGE ONION, FINELY CHOPPED
1 TSP PAPRIKA
2 LARGE PLUM TOMATOES, DICED
2TBS FRESH MINT, FINELY CHOPPED
SALT & PEPPER

Bring the stock to the boil in a large lidded pan with the chick peas and carrot, simmer for 15mins, add the pumpkin, runner beans and pears, reduce the heat and continue to simmer.

While this is cooking, heat the oil in a small pan, gently fry the garlic and almonds for 2 mins, drain, stir in the vinegar and set aside.

Using the same oil and pan, fry the onion until soft, stir in the paprika, add the tomatoes and reduce until thick.

Stir this mixture into the main soup mix, then add the almond mixture and mint, season and stir well.

Serve in bowls with crusty bread.

HEALTHY HANGOVER BROTH

1 LARGE CARROT	6 LARGE TOMATOES
1 LARGE ONION	1/2 CUP OF PEAS
1 FENNEL BULB	1/2 BUNCH SPRING ONIONS
2 STICKS OF CELERY	LARGE BUNCH OF PARSLEY
1 GREEN PEPPER	LOTS OF OLIVE OIL
1 LEEK	SALT AND PEPPER TO TASTE
1 APPLE	A SQUEEZE OF LEMON JUICE
5 CLOVES GARLIC	

1. Finely dice the vegetables, keeping the tomato, peas, spring onion and garlic separate. Mince the garlic.

2. In a pan, combine the diced veg and lots of olive oil. Cook on a low heat and stir every so often for about ten minutes.

3. Add the tomatoes and garlic and cook gently before adding boiling water and boiling for around five minutes.

4. Add the peas, spring onions, parsley, lemon juice and seasoning at the last minute and serve.

PORTOBELLO MUSHROOM SOUP

400G PORTOBELLO MUSHROOMS, CHOPPED (BUTTON OR CHESTNUT WORK WELL TOO)
25G VEGAN SPREAD (MARG)
750ML VEG STOCK
1-2 CLOVES GARLIC, CRUSHED OR FINELY CHOPPED
LARGE HANDFUL PARSLEY LEAVES, ROUGHLY CHOPPED
SALT AND PEPPER

1. In a large pan, melt the spread on a low heat. Add mushrooms and garlic. Cook until mushrooms are just softened. Add stock and simmer gently for 5 minutes.

2. Blend until smooth then add parsley. Season with salt and pepper to taste.

CURRIED SOUP

1 LARGE ROOT VEGETABLE OR SQUASH
1 LARGE ONION
1 TBSP CURRY POWDER
1 STOCK CUBE

Chop veg and onion into small chunks.

Fry until they're caramelised and start sticking when stirred.

Add more oil and the curry powder, fry for a minute.

Add enough water to cover it all and add the stock cube. Put a lid on it and boil for about twenty minutes. Season with salt, blend. Eat.

ONION BHAJI

4 OZ GRAM FLOUR
2 LARGE ONIONS, CHOPPED
1 TSP FRESH CORIANDER, CHOPPED
1/2 TSP TURMERIC
1 TO 2 CHILLIES (TO TASTE), DE-SEEDED AND FINELY CHOPPED
A PINCH OF SALT
1/4 PINT WATER
OIL FOR DEEP-FRYING

Mix all the dry ingredients together, then add the water gradually until you have a thick batter (you may not need to use it all) and mix gently until smooth. Leave to stand for an hour if you have time (for a thicker consistency), or it is ok to use immediately.

Heat the oil. Test if it is hot enough by throwing in a small piece of bread. If it fries immediately, you are ready to go.

Using 2 tablespoons, drop golf ball sized amounts (golf ball sized for crunchy bhajis, or on a lower heat larger amounts can be used) into the oil - deep fry them in batches for 2-3 minutes, until golden brown.

RED LENTIL KOFTE

EQUAL QUANTITIES OF SPLIT RED LENTILS
AND WATER (1 CUP TO 1 CUP)
1 FRESHLY MINCED ONION
2CM PEELED GINGER ROOT, FINELY CHOPPED
CHOPPED FRESH CORIANDER/PARSLEY
APPROX. 750 ML VEGETABLE OIL FOR FRYING
SALT TO TASTE

1. Mix the lentils and water together in equal measures and soak fo
   at least 4 hours, but preferably overnight. The lentils should soa
   most of the liquid up.

2. Blend the lentils, water and onion in a food processor and blit:
   until a thick smooth batter is formed. Add the ginger and
   coriander and blitz until roughly chopped.

3. This batter is best made in advance and left to thicken in the fridg
   but it can be used straight away (if it is too runny to make fritter:
   or quenelles with, I usually drain some of it in a sieve). The batte
   may seem wet but it will hold together as you fry it.

4. Heat the oil in a pan (test the temperature by dropping a smal
   piece of bread in – if it fries quickly, it's hot enough).

5. Using two spoons – the first to scoop, the second to release the
   batter – gently drop dollops of batter into the hot oil. Allow time
   for the oil to seal the outside of the kofte completely (it wil
   unstick itself from the bottom of the pan too) before stirring
   regularly and lowering the heat – cook until golden, strain and
   serve with lemon slices.

6. This is a very versatile recipe, any fresh herbs can be added - curry
   powder is also good. I really like to make them with aromatic
   spices - cardamom and ginger is my favourite. They're also good
   with the addition of red pepper paste or smoked paprika.

FALAFEL

THIS MIDDLE EASTERN CLASSIC IS OFTEN SERVED WITH HUMMUS AND SALAD.

8OZ DRIED CHICKPEAS – SOAK OVERNIGHT (DO NOT BOIL)
1 ONION, ROUGHLY CHOPPED
3 CLOVES OF GARLIC
1 SLICE OF OLD BREAD, ROUGHLY CUBED
A LARGE HANDFUL OF FRESH PARSLEY AND CORIANDER
1 TSP GROUND CUMIN (AND SOME CUMIN SEEDS)
SALT TO TASTE
OIL, FOR FRYING

WEST MIDLANDS
HUNT SABOTEURS

Blend the uncooked chickpeas, garlic, herbs, onion, bread, salt and cumin into a paste. Some people like this very smooth but I like to leave it a little rougher for more crunchiness at the end (I also add sesame seeds and sometimes fennel seeds).

If the mixture is very heavy looking, add a half a tsp bicarbonate of soda.

Mix well with your hands and make into 15-20 patty/falafel shapes or golf ball sized balls. If you wet your hands before putting them in the mix, it won't stick to them.

Drop the shapes into the hot oil (test the heat by dropping a small piece of bread into it - if it fries rapidly, you are ready to go!).

Try to get the whole batch in the oil at the same time so that they cook for the same amount of time. If they stick to the bottom of the pan, wait for the outside to cook solidly then shuffle off the bottom gently (or they will explode!). Stir as they fry and once they are brown, remove and drain.

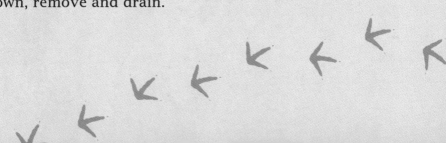

FAJITAS (THANKS TO SOUTHAMPTON HUNT SABOTEURS)

LARGE SOYA CHUNKS
1 FAJITA KIT (VEGAN ONES ARE AVAILABLE IN MOST SUPERMARKETS)
PEPPERS OF ASSORTED COLOURS
SPRING ONION
1 LARGE ONION (RED OR WHITE)
CHILLI PEPPER (OPTIONAL)

1. In a large frying pan, soak the soya chunks in boiling water, add a tablespoon of oil and heat gently until all the liquid has been absorbed.

2. Keep on the heat and add approx. half a cup of oil to the chunks (the water will be absorbed completely and the chunks will begin to fry).

3. Fry the chunks until browned and crisp. Keep stirring to prevent them from sticking to the pan.

4. When the chunks are crispy, remove from the heat, drain any excess oil and leave to one side.

5. Fry the sliced onions, peppers and chillies in a separate pan with a little oil and add the fajita powder flavouring.

6. Stir over a gentle heat and add the drained chunks. When it is cooked to preference, take off the heat and put in a large serving dish.

7. Serve with wraps and salsa. Add lettuce and some crunchy spring onions to taste.

MOZZARELLA

1/4 CUP RAW CASHEWS, SOAKED OVERNIGHT OR BOILED FOR 15 MINUTES
1 CUP AQUAFABA (CHICK PEA BRINE)
2 TBSP TAPIOCA STARCH
2 TSP KAPPA CARRAGEENAN
1 TSP VEGAN LACTIC ACID
1 TSP NUTRITIONAL YEAST
3/4 TSP SALT
6 TBSP REFINED COCONUT OIL, LIQUID

Blend the softened cashews and aquafaba in a high speed blender until smooth. Strain it through a fine mesh sieve to remove any large particles and return to blender. It should be very smooth after blending.

Add the tapioca starch, carrageenan, lactic acid, nutritional yeast and salt, and pulse it in a blender to combine.

Add the coconut oil and blend again very briefly. The mixture will be smooth and thick.

Heat in a medium saucepan over medium-low heat while stirring regularly. It will look quite lumpy as the tapioca starch activates but it will eventually turn smooth and glossy. When it reaches 170°F, it will be done. You will see it begin to bubble around the edges and maintain its thickness.

Pour it into a mould or scoop balls into iced water. Refrigerate for a few hours to fully firm up the cheese before slicing or grating. This cheese is great on pizza or cut into sticks and fried.

*For more recipes that use aquafaba, see the end of the Desserts, Cakes and Sweets section.

BUCKWHEAT FLATBREAD (KUTTU KI PURI)

100G BUCKWHEAT FLOUR (KUTTU) - SET ASIDE 1/4 CUP FOR ROLLING THE PURIS
2 LARGE POTATOES, BOILED AND MASHED
1/2 TEASPOON SALT
1/2 TEASPOON CUMIN SEEDS (JEERA)
1/8 TEASPOON OF RED PEPPER (SWEET PAPRIKA)
LUKEWARM WATER, USE AS NEEDED
OIL FOR FRYING

1. Mix buckwheat flour, cumin seeds, pepper, and salt well. Add potatoes, mix it well. Add warm water as needed to make smooth and pliable dough. Set aside for five minutes.

2. Divide the dough in eight equal parts, oil your palms and roll them into smooth patties.

3. Before rolling the puris out, press both sides of the patties on the dry flour to make them easy to roll.

4. Roll them into six-inch circles. Sprinkle more flour as needed if the puris start sticking to the rolling pin or rolling surface.

5. Heat at least one inch of oil in a frying pan over a medium high heat. To check if oil is ready, drop a small piece of dough into the oil - it should come up slowly.

6. Place one puri at a time in the frying pan and press it with a skimmer. The puris should puff up slowly. Turn the puris over. Puri should be light brownish-grey on both sides.

7. Take the puris out and place them on paper towels to absorb the excess oil.

8. Serve the puris hot, or store in a covered container after they have cooled to room temperature.

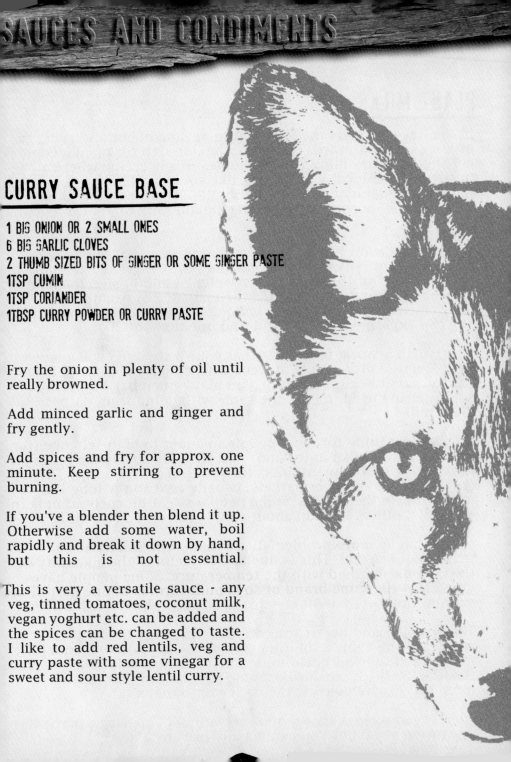

CURRY SAUCE BASE

1 BIG ONION OR 2 SMALL ONES
6 BIG GARLIC CLOVES
2 THUMB SIZED BITS OF GINGER OR SOME GINGER PASTE
1TSP CUMIN
1TSP CORIANDER
1TBSP CURRY POWDER OR CURRY PASTE

Fry the onion in plenty of oil until really browned.

Add minced garlic and ginger and fry gently.

Add spices and fry for approx. one minute. Keep stirring to prevent burning.

If you've a blender then blend it up. Otherwise add some water, boil rapidly and break it down by hand, but this is not essential.

This is very a versatile sauce - any veg, tinned tomatoes, coconut milk, vegan yoghurt etc. can be added and the spices can be changed to taste. I like to add red lentils, veg and curry paste with some vinegar for a sweet and sour style lentil curry.

PLANT MILKS

If you haven't made the jump yet to veganism but are trying to, or are working towards it, the first major step for many people is cutting out dairy milk. When it comes to any recipe where heating is involved, a plant milk like soya is often indistinguishable in taste to dairy milk. If you eat a breakfast cereal in the morning, then trying a plant milk on that is a good first step.

What's important to remember is that there is not only a huge range of plant milks (oat, hemp, almond, soya, rice, hazelnut, coconut etc) but that there are sweetened and unsweetened versions of many of them AND the taste of, for example, an unsweetened soya milk can vary quite a lot from brand to brand. So keep experimenting till you find one that you like.

Also worth bearing in mind is that your taste buds will adapt over a period of a couple of weeks. If you have ever gone from full fat milk to skimmed milk, you may remember how it took some getting used to - it's the same with going from dairy to plant milks.

The hardest thing for most people to adapt to is the change from dairy to plant milks in tea and/or coffee. My advice for tea is just keep trying all the plant milks till you find one you like. There's a good range in all supermarkets, usually next to the long life milks AND in the fridges. Some people swear on coconut milk in tea whilst others rave on about vanilla flavoured rice milk.

Coffee can be more problematic in that plant milks have a tendency to curdle. This is due to two factors - the alkalinity of the coffee combined with the temperature. Some people have noted that the same brand of soya milk curdles in one part of the country but not in another - this is down to the water hardness.

The stronger and hotter the coffee is, the more likely it is to curdle, so the simple solution is to allow the coffee to cool for a minute and then add cold milk. The more cold milk that you add, the less likely it is to curdle. Some people find that they have more success by pouring the coffee onto the milk.

Most vegan recipes that require a plant milk specify a particular one (often soya) but you can usually use any.

CHEESE SAUCE

1/2 CUP UNSWEETENED SOYA MILK
1/2 CUP VEG OIL (SUNFLOWER OR RAPESEED, NOT OLIVE)
LEMON JUICE
ENGLISH MUSTARD
BOUILLON

1. Add lemon to milk and heat on the stove.

2. Add oil slowly while whisking.

3. Add bouillon and mustard to taste.

4. Blend in blender or whisk with high-powered whisk until thick.

5. Add tofu to make it like a spreadable cream cheese. Herbs/garlic are always a good addition.

MAYONNAISE (THANKS TO SOUTH WALES HUNT SABOTEURS)

1 CUP HOT (NOT BOILING) SWEETENED SOYA MILK
1 CUP VEGETABLE OIL
1 CLOVE GARLIC
2 TSP LEMON JUICE
2 TSP CIDER VINEGAR
1 TSP MUSTARD
SALT AND PEPPER

SOUTH WALES
HUNT SABOTEURS

1. Place all the ingredients in a jug.

2. Blend with a hand blender.

3. Chill.

FRESH OREGANO AND ROCKET PESTO

50G FRESH OREGANO
30G FRESH ROCKET
1-2 CLOVES GARLIC, CRUSHED
1/4 TEASPOON SALT, OR TO TASTE
BLACK PEPPER
100ML OLIVE OIL

1. Put all of the ingredients into a blender.

2. Blend until all leaves are finely chopped.

3. Serve with freshly cooked pasta.

SALAD DRESSING

6 TEASPOONS AGAVE SYRUP
4 TEASPOONS WHOLE GRAIN MUSTARD
4 DESSERT SPOONS BALSAMIC VINEGAR
OLIVE OIL
SALT AND PEPPER

1. Put the wholegrain mustard in a jam jar with a lid.

2. Add the agave syrup and balsamic vinegar.

4. Season and stir well.

5. Double the mixture with olive oil and shake well. It keeps for weeks with the lid on.

SATAY SAUCE

1 500G BAG OF SALTED PEANUTS
1/2 TIN OF COCONUT MILK
1 TBSP SOY SAUCE
A THUMB SIZED LUMP OF GINGER
5 CLOVES OF GARLIC
1 ONION
A CHILLI OR TWO TO TASTE
1 TBSP LEMONGRASS PASTE (OPTIONAL)
A SLICE OF TINNED PINEAPPLE (OPTIONAL)

Chop the ginger as small as you can first and roughly chop the onion.

If you have a blender, add all the ingredients and blend till it's thick and mostly smooth.

If you don't have a blender, chop everything very finely, fry the dry ingredients for around five minutes, add the wet ingredients and boil until soft. Keep stirring to make sure it doesn't stick.

This is great for marinating veg or fake meats for barbecue skewers. It can be added to stir fries or added to thicken soups. Chunks of floured and fried 'mock duck' (a fake meat) covered in this and baked are amazing, but deep frying takes a lot of effort so that's really for when you're having people over.

JERK PASTE

1 BUNCH SPRING ONIONS
2 OR 3 SCOTCH BONNET CHILLIES
1 GREEN BELL PEPPER
1 RED BELL PEPPER
6 CLOVES GARLIC
LEAVES FROM 5 SPRIGS THYME
1/2 TSP GROUND ALLSPICE
PINCH GROUND MACE
2 TBSP DARK SOY SAUCE

1. Put everything in a blender and blend. Add water if it's too thick. This is a great marinade for barbecued tofu, but also goes well on veg, as a soup base, or on meat substitutes.

THAI GREEN CURRY PASTE

3 STICKS LEMONGRASS
5CM PIECE OF GALANGAL
15 SMALL SHALLOTS
1 BULB OF GARLIC
4 FRESH KAFFIR LIME LEAVES
6 SMALL GREEN CHILLIES (DIFFERENT KINDS DEPENDING HOW HOT YOU LIKE IT)
A TBSP DARK BROWN SUGAR
2CM OF A BLOCK OF COCONUT CREAM
NEUTRAL FLAVOURED OIL (VEGETABLE OR SUNFLOWER)
A BUNCH THAI BASIL
A SMALL BUNCH CORIANDER
JUICE OF 3 LIMES

1. Chop everything finely, apart from the basil and coriander, then blend to a smooth paste, loosening with oil as needed. Fry the paste, making sure it doesn't stick to the pan, add the herbs and lime juice and blend again.

2. Add salt to store it. If you want to keep it in the fridge, put it in an airtight jar and make sure the mixture is submerged in oil. Keeps for a week or two.

TOFU

Tofu is quite bland and the texture can vary. This is the reason that many people don't like it. What people don't realise is that this is tofu's strength! It's incredibly versatile and capable of absorbing a huge range of flavours by marinating. It's texture varies according to the type and how it's cooked - check our pressing tofu page (p.24) for more information.

TOFU MARINADE

1 BLOCK PRESSED TOFU
3 TBSP DARK SOY SAUCE
2 TBSP LIGHT SOY SAUCE
1 TBSP DARK BROWN SUGAR
1 TBSP FINELY GRATED GINGER (OR GINGER PASTE)
1 TBSP MINCED GARLIC (OR GARLIC PASTE)
2 FINELY MINCED HOT CHILLIES (OR A SPOON OF YOUR FAVOURITE CHILLI SAUCE)
3 TBSP LIME JUICE (OR LESS IF YOU LIKE IT LESS TANGY)
1 TBSP TOASTED SESAME OR PEANUT OIL

Mix all the ingredients apart from the tofu (it's easiest is to put them in an empty jam jar and shake it up).

Slice the tofu into whatever size you want it and put it in a shallow container in one layer.

Pour the marinade on to the tofu and leave it for as long as possible - overnight in the fridge or, if you're terrible at planning in advance, an hour will do. If the tofu isn't fully submerged then turn it over at least once to make sure that all sides get a good covering.

Try the tofu cut into thick steaks and barbecued or fried. A George Foreman-type grill also works well, as does baking or a conventional grill. If you cut the tofu into dice and bake them, they make a nice topping for salads in a packed lunch.

Pressed tofu also works well as a paneer substitute.

GENERAL TOMATO SAUCE

2 WHITE ONIONS
2 CARROTS
2 STICKS CELERY
1 RED BELL PEPPER
4 CLOVES GARLIC
2 BAY LEAVES
20 OR SO TWISTS OF BLACK PEPPER
LARGE PINCH SALT
1 TSP SUGAR
4 TBSP OLIVE OIL
4 TINS CHOPPED TOMATOES

1. Finely dice the veg and cook gently in the olive oil, with the pepper and bay leaves, on a low heat for about 20mins .

2. Stir until the veg are cooked, then add everything else and simmer on a medium heat for at least 40mins. Stir every so often to make sure it doesn't stick.

3. If using on pasta, add fresh basil to taste.

4. If using as a bolognaise or lasagne base sauce, add veggie mince. Frozen mince can be added straight in. Dried mince must be soaked first.

5. If using as a pizza base sauce, cook the sauce for longer until it thickens further and add dried Italian herbs.

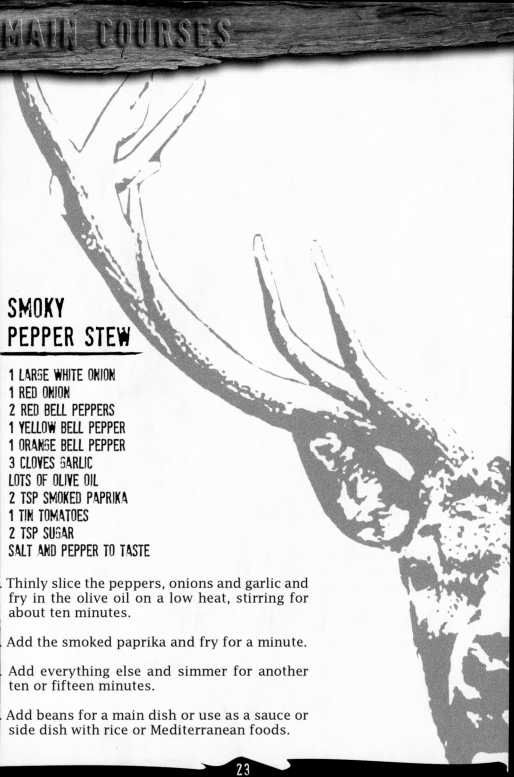

SMOKY PEPPER STEW

1 LARGE WHITE ONION
1 RED ONION
2 RED BELL PEPPERS
1 YELLOW BELL PEPPER
1 ORANGE BELL PEPPER
3 CLOVES GARLIC
LOTS OF OLIVE OIL
2 TSP SMOKED PAPRIKA
1 TIN TOMATOES
2 TSP SUGAR
SALT AND PEPPER TO TASTE

. Thinly slice the peppers, onions and garlic and fry in the olive oil on a low heat, stirring for about ten minutes.

. Add the smoked paprika and fry for a minute.

. Add everything else and simmer for another ten or fifteen minutes.

. Add beans for a main dish or use as a sauce or side dish with rice or Mediterranean foods.

PRESSING TOFU

Lots of people say they don't like tofu. The secret is to make it firmer and give it lots of flavour by using a marinade (see page xx) so that it becomes a totally different thing to the plain and soft stuff that they may have tried.

Freezing tofu helps remove some water so if it's ever on offer, buy in bulk to freeze - you'll only be improving it.

When you decide to use it:

1. Wrap it in kitchen paper, put it in the microwave to defrost.

2. Microwave on high for a couple of minutes.

Both of the above steps help but aren't obligatory. The pressing is the important part:

3. Place your tofu on a chopping board and put something round it to soak up any water (otherwise it'll go all over your kitchen worktop).

4. Place another board on top of the tofu. If you've got a small but heavy wooden chopping board, this is best as wide ones can overbalance. Put a couple of tins on top (or anything heavy - some people use weight training weights for super firm tofu!). Make sure it's central or you can end up with wonky tofu and tins all over your floor.

5. Leave it as long as you can. Pressing the tofu overnight is best but even ten minutes makes a difference. Now you're ready to marinade it and cook how you like.

USE THAT GEORGE FOREMAN GRILL!

An easy way to cook your marinated tofu is to use a George Foreman grill. Marinade the tofu according to the recipe, place in the George Foreman grill for 15 minutes and you will be rewarded with a delicious chewy exterior.

SWEET CHILLI TOFU (THANKS TO GLOS AGAINST BADGER SHOOTING)

400G TOFU
1 RED ONION
3 CLOVES OF GARLIC
2 SWEET PEPPERS
6 TBSP OF SWEET CHILLI SAUCE
1 TBSP OF HOT WATER
SALT AND PEPPER
4 BAY LEAVES

Squeeze the excess water out of the tofu (see page xx) and cube it before baking for 30 minutes at 150 degrees with a couple of tablespoons of olive oil. Use a lasagne dish or baking tray.

Take the (slightly golden) baked tofu out of the oven and add the finely sliced onion.

Mix 6 tablespoons of sweet chilli sauce with 1 tablespoon of boiling water and pour over the tofu and onion before stirring well.

Chop the peppers and add them with the pressed garlic cloves and 4 bay leaves, stir again. Season to taste.

Return to the oven for 45 minutes – stirring once or twice.

BEEF-Y VEGETABLE PIE (THANKS TO SHEFFIELD HUNT SABOTEURS)

ASSORTED VEGETABLES, E.G. POTATOES, SQUASH, ROOT VEG ETC
2 LEEKS
2 ONIONS
2 CLOVES OF GARLIC
100G LENTILS
1 TEASPOON CUMIN
A FEW TWISTS OF BLACK PEPPER
1 TEASPOON PAPRIKA
CORIANDER
ROSEMARY
RED WINE/GRAVY GRANULES
TINNED CHOPPED TOMATOES
PASTRY (SEE CREAMY MUSHROOM AND LEEK PIE, PAGE 30)

1. Fry onions/leeks until transparent, then add a few cloves of garlic

2. Add potatoes/squash/any veg you may be using that'll take a while to cook.

3. Once that's had a head start, add whatever other veg you may be using and give it a good simmer, adding cumin, pepper, coriander and paprika (or some of that "steak seasoning" you can get).

4. When it's all starting to cook, add some lentils (as if you were making dhal), give 'em a stir and add a tin (or more!) of chopped tomatoes, then add water to help the veg cook! It turns out nicer if you use more tomato than water, but you can always cook the liquid off at the end – if you have TVP chunks/soya mince or owt like that, add it here!

5. Add the red wine/gravy granules and herbs, spices and salt to taste and keep simmering it till you get some lovely mush.

6. Roll your pastry out so it'll hang over the edge of the tin, stick it in a greased tin, add the filling and a pastry lid or put stuffing on top

ROAST DINNER

AS AN ALTERNATIVE TO THE TRADITIONAL NUT ROAST, YOU CAN USE THIS RECIPE OR THE BEEF-Y VEGETABLE PIE RECIPE.

CHESTNUT PASTRY BAKE

ABOUT TWO HANDFULS OF COOKED CHESTNUTS (TINNED OR FRESH)
ABOUT THREE HANDFULS OF MUSHROOMS
1 BIG WHITE ONION
2 RED ONIONS
1/2 BOTTLE OF RED WINE
1 VEG STOCK CUBE
A SPRIG OF ROSEMARY
A HANDFUL OF BREADCRUMBS
1 TBSP VEGAN GRAVY GRANULES
1 BLOCK OF READY-MADE PUFF PASTRY
(IF YOU'RE COOKING FOR LOTS OF PEOPLE, USE SOME CHEAP VEGAN STUFFING TO BULK IT OUT)

. Chop the red onions into slices and fry until caramelised, add a teaspoon of sugar if you're impatient, it makes them brown faster. Dice the white onion and add to the red ones, fry and stir until translucent.

. Chop and add the mushrooms to the onions. Fry gently until they've reduced in size.

. Chop and add the chestnuts and rosemary and put everything apart from the breadcrumbs and stuffing, if you're using it, in the pan. Boil it for a bit, until it's reduced by about an inch? Keep stirring so it doesn't stick.

. Add your breadcrumbs to dry it out and cook until a doughy texture is achieved. Mix thoroughly.

. If you're using stuffing mix, make it to the packet instructions and then add to the other ingredients. It should be a thick consistency when you roll into a sausage shape and wrap in the rolled out pastry. Bake on a baking tray until golden (approx 30 or 40 minutes) at 200°C.

ROAST DINNER (CONT'D)

POSH PARSNIPS

ONE PARSNIP PER PERSON
STOCK
OIL
2 TBSP MAPLE SYRUP
2 TBSP SESAME SEEDS

1. Boil the parsnips in the dissolved stock for about fifteen minutes. Put them in a roasting tin with plenty of oil and roast at 200°C for around twenty minutes.

2. Remove most of the oil (use it for other stuff), add the maple syrup and sesame seeds and stir until the parsnips are covered, then roast for another ten minutes and serve.

RED CABBAGE

1 RED CABBAGE
1 LARGE COOKING APPLE
½ HANDFUL RAISINS (OPTIONAL)
1 CUP RED WINE
SALT
1 PINCH ALLSPICE
1 PINCH CINNAMON

1. Chop everything finely and put in a dish. Cover with foil and cook in the oven for about half an hour at 200°C. Stir before serving.

CARROT AND SWEDE MASH

CARROTS AND SWEDE
OIL/MARG

1. Peel and chop equal amounts of carrot and swede. Boil until mashable then add salt and a pinch of nutmeg. Mash with vegan margarine or oil.

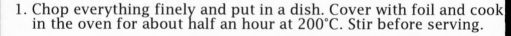

ROAST DINNER (CONT'D)

PROPER ROAST POTATOES

PLENTY OF OIL
TWO OR THREE POTATOES PER PERSON
TWO ONIONS
ONE HEAD OF GARLIC
VEG STOCK
SALT
1 TSP MUSTARD
1 TSP SUGAR
A SPRIG OF ROSEMARY

Peel and chop the potatoes into thirds. Peel the onions and half of the garlic. Put everything (except the unpeeled half head of garlic and the oil) into a pan of cold stock and bring it to the boil. Boil for about 15 minutes until the potatoes are soft. Drain and save the water for gravy.

Add the veg to hot oil in a roasting tin (the oil should come halfway up the spuds). Roast for about 20 minutes at 200°C, turning halfway through. When cooked drain most of the oil off and roast them for another ten or fifteen minutes.

GRAVY

1 BIG RED ONION
1 BIG MUSHROOM, OR A FEW SMALL ONES
½ BOTTLE RED WINE
LEFTOVER STOCK FROM YOUR VEG
2 TSP CORNFLOUR

Chop the onion and fry until browned. Finely chop and add the mushrooms, fry gently then add the red wine. Cook on a low heat until it's reduced by at least half and dilute with a ladle of stock.

In a separate cup, mix the cornflour with some cold water, pour the thickener slowly into the gravy (use a whisk to avoid lumps or blend to remove any lumps) and boil until thickened.

CREAMY MUSHROOM AND LEEK PIE

THIS MAKES AN AVERAGE PIE FOR ABOUT 4/5 PEOPLE (BIG SLICES)

FOR THE FILLING:
OIL FOR FRYING
1 LARGE LEEK, CHOPPED INTO SMALL PIECES
1 CLOVE GARLIC, FINELY CHOPPED
20 MUSHROOMS, WASHED AND SLICED
1 CUP CASHEW NUTS – PROCESS WITH 2 CUPS WATER IN YOUR LIQUIDIZER UNTIL IT
RESEMBLES SINGLE CREAM OR ANY PLANT-BASED MILK (THOUGH CASHEW MILK IS THICKER)
1 TBSP NUTRITIONAL YEAST
1 TSP VEGETABLE STOCK POWDER OR A STOCK CUBE
SALT TO TASTE
SLICED VEGAN SAUSAGES (OPTIONAL)

FOR THE DOUGH:
500G FLOUR
50G OF MARG

1. Add the marg to the flour and turn it into breadcrumb-like stuff with your finger tips. When you get a bowl of mixture that resembles bread crumbs, slowly add water and make a doughy ball. Knead it for 10/15 minutes, then leave till it's needed.

2. Fry leeks in oil in a large saucepan for a couple of minutes or so, until slightly transparent.

3. Stir in the mushrooms and garlic, and lower the heat. Cook until juicy!

4. Add the remaining ingredients, except for the cashew cream (and sausages, if you're using them).

5. Make sure your veggies are totally cooked, and then add your cream a little at a time.

CREAMY MUSHROOM AND LEEK PIE (CONT'D)

Keep a low heat setting, allow the filling to thicken a little, and then add the remaining cream – again simmering until it thickens.

Taste for salt, then allow your filling to cool down.

Meanwhile roll out your dough on a clean surface with flour on.

Make pie! Extra points for inventive pie decoration!

COURGETTE FRITTERS WITH SOURED CREAM

1 LARGE COURGETTE, GRATED
1/2 TSP SALT
2 LARGE GARLIC CLOVES, MINCED
1 TSP BAKING POWDER
2 OZ WHEAT FLOUR (OR GRAM FLOUR)
1/2 TSP DRIED CORIANDER
1/2 TSP ONION POWDER
1/4 TSP FRESHLY GROUND BLACK PEPPER
1 TBSP OLIVE/MUSTARD/SUNFLOWER OIL

KERNOW

HUNT SABS

For the soured cream:

1. Soak 4 oz cashews in water for at least a couple of hours, then add them to a blender with 1tsp lemon juice, a few drops of cider vinegar and salt to taste.

2. Blend until smooth, adding water to get the right consistency.

For the fritters:

1. Sprinkle some salt over the grated courgette, allow to sit in a colander for about an hour to remove some water. Squeeze out any excess water by wrapping it in a clean tea towel and rub off excess salt.

2. Put the courgettes in a large bowl and add in the minced garlic, flour, coriander, onion powder and black pepper. Stir well to form a loose dough-like texture.

3. Form into balls and press gently to flatten, ready for cooking in batches.

4. Heat the oil in a large pan over medium heat. Cook until golden (about 5 minutes), then flip and cook for another few minutes until that side has also browned lightly.

TOFU QUICHE

1 ROLL PRE-MADE PASTRY
1 500G BLOCK SILKEN TOFU (NORMAL WORKS TOO)
1/2 TBSP VEGAN BOUILLON POWDER OR A STOCK CUBE
1 TBSP DARK SOY SAUCE
2 CLOVES GARLIC
1 TBSP WHOLEGRAIN MUSTARD
2 TBSP NUTRITIONAL YEAST (OPTIONAL)
LOTS OF GROUND BLACK PEPPER

DERBY SABS

Line a greased quiche tin with the pre-rolled pastry. Prick the base a few times with a fork. Cover with greaseproof paper and dried rice or beans (or fancy baking beans if you have them) and blind bake as per packet instructions (or if you use home-made pastry blind bake till it's cooked on the bottom but not too brown on the edges).

While this is baking, blend all your other ingredients.

For a plain quiche, put the filling in the base and bake for about fifteen minutes on 180°C, or until firm to the touch.

For a more colourful quiche, add veg such as peas, asparagus and chopped parsley. Red pepper works nicely, especially if you spread the pastry base with harissa before adding the tofu filling. Fake meats like bacon, chorizo etc. work well too.

RED LENTIL AND BUTTERNUT SQUASH BURGERS

MAKES 4 BURGERS

1/3 LB DRY RED LENTILS
1/2 BUTTERNUT SQUASH
6 SPRING ONIONS
2 CLOVES GARLIC
1 TSP SMOKED PAPRIKA
1 TSP CAYENNE PEPPER
1 1/2 TABLESPOONS GLUTEN-FREE FLOUR (OR GRAM OR RICE FLOUR)
FINELY CHOPPED CORIANDER STALKS AND LEAVES

1. Boil the lentils in the same amount of unsalted water (measure them in a cup and add the same amount of water) until they're tender, not mushy and overcooked. Drain and allow to cool in a colander.

2. Chop the squash into large chunks, place in a bowl and coat in oil – take them out individually (to avoid all the oil going on the baking tray) and place onto a baking tray and roast for approx. 20-25mins at 200°C.

3. Remove from oven. Once cooled, chop into small dice and set aside.

4. Mix all the remaining ingredients with the squash and lentils, mix thoroughly – hands are best at this stage – and shape into 4 burgers. Leave to set in the fridge for at least an hour.

5. To serve, gently fry the burgers until browned and hot all the way through – be gentle with them or bake in the oven.

6. Serve with crispy potato wedges and salad.

QUARTERPOUNDER BEET BURGERS
(THANKS TO CAMBRIDGE HUNT SABOTEURS)

EVERYONE LOVES BURGERS AND THIS IS A FINE UPSTANDING BURGER. MAKE THESE GUYS BIG, QUARTER POUNDER SIZE! TO MAKE THESE MORE FAST-FOODY, TOP WITH SHREDDED LETTUCE, SLICED DILL PICKLES, FINELY DICED ONION AND KETCHUP. YOU CAN ADD A LAYER OF AVOCADO INSTEAD OF A VEGAN CHEESE.

IF YOU'D LIKE TO MAKE THESE GLUTEN-FREE, JUST USE GLUTEN-FREE BREADCRUMBS. IF YOU'D LIKE TO USE A DIFFERENT NUT BUTTER, WE RECOMMEND CASHEW. USE A FOOD PROCESSOR TO MAKE THESE QUICKLY.

1 1/4 CUPS COOKED, COOLED RICE
1 CUP COOKED BROWN OR GREEN LENTILS, COOLED, DRAINED WELL
1 CUP SHREDDED BEETROOT
1/2 TEASPOON SALT
FRESH BLACK PEPPER
1 TEASPOON THYME
1/2 TEASPOON GROUND FENNEL (OR WHOLE FENNEL SEED)
1 TEASPOON DRY MUSTARD
3 TABLESPOONS FINELY CHOPPED ONION
2 CLOVES GARLIC, MINCED
2 TABLESPOONS SMOOTH ALMOND BUTTER
1/2 CUP FINE BREADCRUMBS
OLIVE OIL FOR THE PAN

CAMBRIDGE HUNT SABS. PROTECTING WILDLIFE. FOXING UP THE HUNTERS' FUN.

. Shred beets with the shredder attachment of your food processor, then set aside. Change the attachment to a metal blade. Pulse the brown rice, shredded beetroot and lentils about 15 to 20 times, until the mixture comes together, but still has texture.

. Now transfer to a mixing bowl and add all of the remaining ingredients. Use your hands to mix well. Place the mixture in the fridge for half an hour to chill.

. Preheat a heavy pan over medium-high heat!

QUARTERPOUNDER BEET BURGERS (CONT'D)

4. Now form the patties... make them big!

5. Pour a very thin layer of oil into the pan and cook patties for about 12 minutes, flipping occasionally.

6. Do two at a time if your pan isn't big enough. You want to get the burger charred - not burnt, but charred.

7. Serve immediately with all the trimmings!

POTATO SALAD

500G BABY NEW POTATOES OR SALAD POTATOES
3 CARROTS
3 SPRING ONIONS OR A HANDFUL OF FRESH CHIVES
FRESH PARSLEY
VEGAN MAYONNAISE (SEE PAGE 17)

NOTTS HUNT SABS

. Boil the new potatoes for 15-20 minutes so they drop off a sharp knife but are still firm.

. Chop up the carrots and the potatoes into bite-sized chunks.

. Add the spring onions/chives and parsley (all chopped finely).

. Mix in 6 tablespoons of vegan mayo, with salt and pepper to taste.

PAN HAGGERTY

FINELY SLICED POTATOES
SHREDDED LEEKS OR FINELY SLICED ONIONS
GARLIC
VEG OF YOUR CHOICE
VEG STOCK
SWEET PAPRIKA
SALT AND PEPPER
SUNFLOWER OIL

THREE
COUNTIES
HUNT
SABS

1. With a mandolin veg slicer (or with a knife), finely slice a mixture of vegetables. The main ingredient in this recipe is potatoes, with leeks and other veg in the layers. Keep all the veg in separate piles and move fast to stop the potatoes going black.

2. If you're going to add other sliced veg in the layers, start with the hardest (root veg etc.) at the bottom and layers of softer stuff (like tomatoes) towards the top.

3. Start with some oil in the bottom of a pan or dish that can go on the hob and in the oven (though baking this dish is not essential!).

4. Begin with a layer of potatoes around the edges and overlap slightly into the centre, making sure to leave a circular space (in all the layers) in the middle.

5. Season lightly, add a layer of onion/leek/garlic and cover with a layer of potatoes. Continue layering all the way to the top of the dish (adding your veg of choice, or sticking to the traditional leek and potato). Make sure to end in a layer of potatoes and then dust with sweet or smoked paprika.

6. Cover with vegetable stock or water and put a lid on, boil until a knife goes through all the layers, remove the lid and cook off some of the liquid before putting in the oven on a high heat until the top goes crispy and brown. If your dish isn't oven proof the residual liquids make a great gravy/sauce.

NUTTY PASTA (THANKS TO SOMERSET AGAINST THE BADGER CULL)

6 OZ SPAGHETTI OR NOODLES
1 ONION, FINELY CHOPPED
2 TBS COLD PRESSED RAPESEED OIL
1/4 PT TOMATO JUICE (CAN OF CHOPPED TOMATOES)
3 TBPS CRUNCHY PEANUT BUTTER
1 TSP YEAST EXTRACT OR SOY SAUCE
1 TSP MADRAS CURRY POWDER

Somerset
Against the
Badger
Cull

FOR GARNISH:
FEW SALTED PEANUTS, A FEW LEMON TWISTS, A FEW RED AND GREEN PEPPERS (THINLY
SLICED AND LIGHTLY FRIED)

Boil noodles or spaghetti until tender and then drain.

Whilst they're cooking, fry onion in oil until golden brown.

Stir in tomato juice, peanut butter, yeast extract (or soy sauce), curry powder and more tomato juice, if needed, to make a smooth sauce.

Drain the noodles/spaghetti and serve with the sauce.

Garnish with peanuts, lemon twist and peppers, or anything else you fancy.

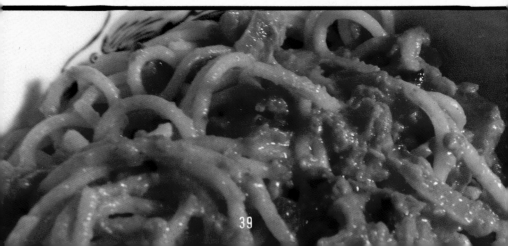

STUFFED AUBERGINES

2 MEDIUM ONIONS, CHOPPED
1/2-3/4 CUP OLIVE OIL
2 GARLIC CLOVES, CRUSHED
3 MEDIUM TOMATOES, PEELED AND CHOPPED
4 TBSP CHOPPED PARSLEY
1 TBSP CHOPPED OF FRESH MINT OR 1/2 TEASPOON DRIED MINT, CRUMBLED
SALT AND PEPPER
2 MEDIUM AUBERGINES
1 TSP SUGAR
2 TBSP FRESH LEMON JUICE

1. Sauté the onions lightly in a little oil before adding the garlic, tomatoes, parsley, salt and pepper. Cook until it comes together as a very thick stew (no liquid), then stir in the mint.

2. Cut the stem ends from each aubergine and cut in half lengthwise. Make 3 lengthwise slits, almost from end to end, cutting into the flesh about 1 inch deep.

3. Fry the aubergine face down (skin side up) in about half a cup of olive oil, it needs to stew a bit. Turn the aubergines and fry the other side once the flesh side is well browned. Remove them from what's left of the oil (most of it will have been soaked up) and drain on some kitchen towel or in a colander so the juices can be collected – this should take about 15 minutes.

4. Preheat oven to 180°C.

5. Open the slits in the aubergine and push as much of the tomato mixture in as possible, then place alongside each other in a well-fitting oven dish (too much space around the aubergines will reduce the juices too much and there will be nothing to mop up with the crunchy bread at the end).

6. Sprinkle with sugar, lemon juice, parsley and drizzle with the remaining oil. Bake for 40 minutes, or until tender – the aubergines will melt and make a lot of juices. Serve with lots of crusty bread.

RICE AND BEANS

1 TIN KIDNEY BEANS
1/3 BLOCK OF CREAMED COCONUT
5 SPRING ONIONS
LEAVES FROM ABOUT FIVE SPRIGS OF THYME OR 1/2 TSP DRIED THYME
1 GARLIC CLOVE
1 CUP RICE
A PINCH GROUND ALLSPICE
SALT TO TASTE
1 CHILLI (OPTIONAL)

. Cook the kidney beans for ten minutes in the water from the tin. The liquid should go nice and red.

. Chop the spring onions into small pieces and add the rest of the ingredients to the pan with the beans.

. Cover everything with about an inch of water over at the top. If you're using an electric hob, boil for about five minutes, then put a lid on and turn the heat off. Don't touch it. As the hob cools down, it should keep soaking up the liquid until there's none left (draining the rice wastes all the added flavours).

. If you're using a gas cooker, cook on the lowest setting possible and keep an eye on it. It's done when the water is gone and there are holes showing between the rice and beans on the top.

. Add salt to taste - it's best salty.

NORTHANTS
HUNT SABOTEURS

MOUSSAKA

FOR THE BASE:
HALF THE QUANTITY OF GENERAL TOMATO SAUCE (SEE PAGE 22)
2 AUBERGINES
1 LARGE POTATO
4 PORTIONS OF VEGAN MINCE OR COOKED GREEN LENTILS
1 TSP DRIED MINT
1/2 TSP CINNAMON
1/2 BOTTLE RED WINE (VEGAN)

FOR THE TOPPING:
1 PACKET TOFU
2 TBSP LEMON JUICE
SOY MILK TO THIN
2 TBSP NUTRITIONAL YEAST
A SMALL GRATE OF NUTMEG

1. Slice the potato into finger-thick rounds, boil for 5 minutes, coat with oil, season with salt and cover the base of a deep lasagne dish. Place in the oven at 180°C for 10 minutes.

2. Fry the mince or lentils with the cinnamon for a minute or two (or as per instructions for mince). Then add the red wine and simmer on a low heat for about ten minutes until it's reduced by half. Remove the potatoes from the oven.

3. Combine the tomato sauce, mince/lentil and wine mix with the mint and heat through.

4. Slice the aubergine into rounds.

5. Cover the potato with a layer of sauce. Cover with a layer of sliced aubergines, then sauce, then aubergine until all the ingredients are used up.

6. For the topping, blend all the topping ingredients and pour over the layered mixture and bake for half an hour at 200°C.

VEGETABLE CHILLI

1 TSP CUMIN
1 TSP CHILLI POWDER
1/2 TSP SMOKED PAPRIKA
1/4 TSP CINNAMON
1/2 TSP MIXED HERBS
4 SQUARES DARK CHOCOLATE
1 WHITE ONION
4 CLOVES GARLIC
1/2 PUNNET OF MUSHROOMS
2 BELL PEPPERS OF ANY COLOUR
1 COURGETTE
2 TINS OF BEANS. MOST KINDS WORK.
1/2 QUANTITY OF BASE TOMATO SAUCE (SEE PAGE 22)
SQUEEZE OF LIME JUICE
HANDFUL OF CHOPPED FRESH CORIANDER (OPTIONAL)

1. Dice all the veg. Leave chunky if you like.

2. Brown the onion in the oil, then add all the spices and fry for about a minute while stirring.

3. Add all the veg and stir fry for about five minutes.

4. Add the rest of the ingredients apart from the lime juice and coriander and boil for about ten minutes, then add the lime and coriander and serve.

5. Serve with rice or in wraps with salsa, guacamole, salad or hummus side dishes.

SAMBAR

2 TSP CORIANDER SEEDS
1 TBSP RED LENTILS
4 DRIED RED CHILLIES
1/4 TSP CUMIN
1/4 TSP FENUGREEK SEEDS
1/2 CUP YELLOW SPLIT PEAS
1 TBSP TAMARIND PASTE
WHATEVER VEG YOU FANCY – E.G. ONION, CARROT, OKRA, AUBERGINE,
RADISH, TOMATO, GARLIC, CUCUMBER AND SPINACH
1 TSP BROWN MUSTARD SEEDS
20 CURRY LEAVES
1 PINCH ASAFOETIDA
SALT

1. Dry fry the red lentils and the chillies, stirring for about a minute on high heat.

2. Add the coriander seeds and dry fry for another minute or so.

3. Add the other spices and dry fry for another 30 seconds.

4. Blend or combine it all in a pestle and mortar. The end product should ideally be a powder.

5. Put the sambar powder aside and boil the split peas in about four cups of water for about half an hour until they are soft and can be mashed smoothly in the water.

6. Dice your chosen veg and add to the peas with sambar powder. At this stage add the tamarind paste and boil until the veg is tender.

7. In another pan, fry the mustard seeds in hot oil until they pop, then add the curry leaves and asafoetida.

8. Fry for a minute and put it in your soup. Stir through and serve.

9. Add salt to taste.

POTATO MASALA

4 OR 5 LARGE POTATOES
2 LARGE ONIONS DICED
1 SMALL HANDFUL URAD DAL
1 TSP GINGER PASTE
2 TSP BROWN MUSTARD SEEDS
3 GREEN CHILLIES
1/2 TSP TURMERIC
A PINCH ASAFOETIDA
20 OR SO CURRY LEAVES
OIL
SALT

W. Yorkshire
Sabs

Peel and chop the potatoes into medium dice. Boil until they're soft all the way through. Drain, but save about 4 tbsp of the water.

Fry the dal until it is darker brown than it was, then add half the mustard seeds until they pop.

Chop the green chillies in half, add them to the pan with the ginger, the turmeric and half of the curry leaves.

After a minute of stirring, add the onions and fry and stir until they're translucent.

Add the cooked potatoes and the saved water. Cover and simmer, stirring every so often to make sure the mix doesn't stick to the bottom. After about seven minutes the potatoes should be cooked down well.

In a small frying pan, heat some oil and add the rest of the mustard seeds. When they've all popped, add the rest of the curry leaves and the asafoetida. Fry for a minute, don't let it burn.

Add the mix to the potatoes and stir well. Add salt to taste.

Serve with dosa and chutneys. Can also be served as a side to any curry.

CREAMY SPINACH PUFF PASTRY HEAVEN

1 BLOCK OF VEGAN PUFF PASTRY, DEFROSTED
25G VEGAN SPREAD
1 ONION, DICED
150G MUSHROOMS, CHOPPED
200G FRESH SPINACH
1-2 CLOVES GARLIC
200ML CARTON SOYA CREAM
1/2 VEGETABLE STOCK CUBE
1/2 TSP GROUND NUTMEG

1. Set oven to gas mark 7 (or equivalent).

2. In a saucepan, melt spread on a medium heat and fry the onion for 5-6 minutes until softened.

3. Add mushrooms and garlic and cook for a further 3-4 minutes.

4. Add the soya cream and spinach, lower heat and cook for a few more minutes until the spinach has wilted.

5. Stir in the nutmeg and season with pepper.

6. Roll out the puff pastry and place on baking tray (you may wish to crimp up the edges to contain the topping).

7. Spread the spinach mixture onto the pastry base and bake for 20-25 minutes until pastry is golden.

8. This is good served with new potatoes in a mustard dressing and steamed greens.

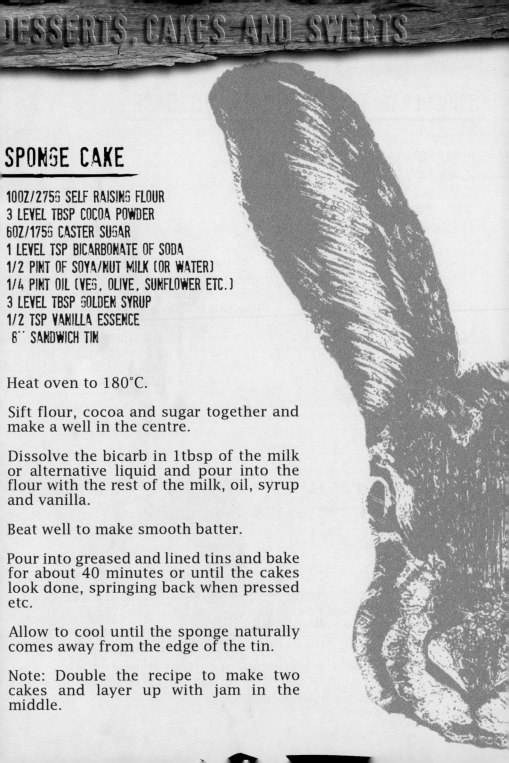

SPONGE CAKE

10OZ/275G SELF RAISING FLOUR
3 LEVEL TBSP COCOA POWDER
6OZ/175G CASTER SUGAR
1 LEVEL TSP BICARBONATE OF SODA
1/2 PINT OF SOYA/NUT MILK (OR WATER)
1/4 PINT OIL (VEG, OLIVE, SUNFLOWER ETC.)
3 LEVEL TBSP GOLDEN SYRUP
1/2 TSP VANILLA ESSENCE
 8″ SANDWICH TIN

Heat oven to 180°C.

Sift flour, cocoa and sugar together and make a well in the centre.

Dissolve the bicarb in 1tbsp of the milk or alternative liquid and pour into the flour with the rest of the milk, oil, syrup and vanilla.

Beat well to make smooth batter.

Pour into greased and lined tins and bake for about 40 minutes or until the cakes look done, springing back when pressed etc.

Allow to cool until the sponge naturally comes away from the edge of the tin.

Note: Double the recipe to make two cakes and layer up with jam in the middle.

CHOCOLATE TORTE WITH BISCUIT BASE

1 PACKET OF GINGER BISCUITS
1/2 CUP OF VEGAN MARGARINE
2 RIPE AVOCADOS
2 500G BARS OF DARK CHOCOLATE
3 TBSP ICING SUGAR
(1 MINCED CHILLI FOR CHILLI CHOCOLATE OR A PINCH OF SEA SALT FOR SALTED CHOCOLATE)

1. Crush the biscuits and add to the melted margarine. Combine well, then press the mix into the base of a (greased) loose-bottom cake tin or something similar. Chill in the fridge until firm to the touch.

2. Melt the chocolate and let it cool a little. Blend the avocados (make sure they are not cold). Mix the avocado and icing sugar into the chocolate until it's smooth. If the chocolate splits, blend it all together rapidly. Pour it onto the chilled base and leave in the fridge for an hour or two until set.

NEARLY ICE CREAM

2 RIPE BANANAS, SLICED THINLY
2 TBSP PEANUT BUTTER

1. Freeze the sliced bananas for at least a few hours, then blend with the peanut butter.

2. You can also make a delicious sorbet by replacing the peanut butter with a couple of very ripe mangoes, blended and placed in the freezer until just starting to freeze. Blend the mangoes with the frozen bananas.

APRICOT PASTRIES

420G CAN OF APRICOT HALVES IN SYRUP
6 READY ROLLED PUFF PASTRY SHEETS, CUT TO 20 X 10CM RECTANGLES
250G OF MARZIPAN
FLAKED ALMONDS TO SPRINKLE

Pour syrup from a tin of apricots into a saucepan and bring to the boil. After 2-3 mins, when it starts to thicken, remove and cool.

Roll and cut the marzipan so that you have 6 rectangles that are each slightly smaller than the pastry rectangles and place them on top of the pastry.

Place the pastries onto a baking sheet, place two apricot halves, cut side down, (or slices) onto each pastry then bake in the oven at 220°C (425°F), gas mark 7 for 15-20 minutes until golden brown.

Brush with the syrup as soon as they come out of the oven.

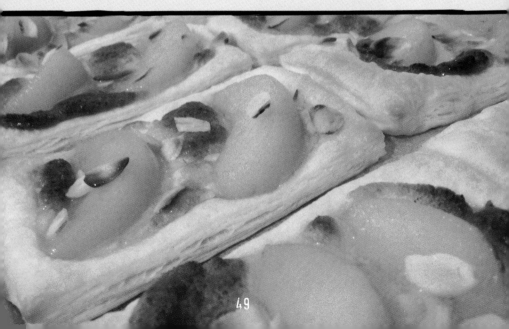

PEANUT COOKIES

170G MARGARINE
90G WHITE SUGAR
90G DARK BROWN SUGAR
165G PEANUT BUTTER
260G PLAIN FLOUR
1/2 TSP BICARBONATE OF SODA
PINCH OF SALT
1 TBSP OF LEMON RIND

1. With a hand blender blend everything except flour and bicarb.

2. Sift in flour and bicarb and fold in to mix.

3. Turn oven on 180 degrees

4. Roll into balls a bit smaller than 2 inches in diameter, then place onto a baking sheet and press gently down with a fork in two directions to make a crisscross pattern. Allow for space between each cookie.

5. Bake for 12-15 minutes at 180°C.

BANANA ENERGY CAKE
(THANKS TO BEDS AND BUCKS HUNT SABOTEURS)

225G PLAIN FLOUR
3 HEAPED TEASPOONS BAKING POWDER
100G BROWN SUGAR
3 TEASPOONS CINNAMON OR MIXED SPICE
3 RIPE BANANAS
75G VITALITE OR OTHER NON-DAIRY MARGARINE
VEGAN CHOC CHIPS
RAISINS
WALNUTS

Blend up the bananas with the margarine.

Add everything else and mix well. Add a dash of soya milk if it becomes too sticky.

Chuck in some choc chips, then a few more for good measure, along with some raisins and broken up walnuts.

Pour mixture into a suitable loaf tin with a baking paper liner and sprinkle the top with a little more brown sugar.

Bake in the oven at 200°C until dark golden brown and crusty, and there's no residue on the skewer if you stab it.

PEANUT BUTTER FUDGE

125G MARGARINE
500G DARK BROWN SUGAR
120ML PLANT MILK
250G CRUNCHY PEANUT BUTTER
1 VANILLA POD, SEEDS ONLY
500G ICING SUGAR

DEVON HUNT SABS

1. Melt the margarine in a saucepan over a medium heat.

2. Stir in the brown sugar and milk, and bring to the boil for 2-3 minutes without stirring.

3. Remove from the heat and stir in the peanut butter and vanilla seeds.

4. Place the icing sugar in a large bowl and pour the hot margarine and sugar mixture on top. Using a wooden spoon, beat the mixture until smooth.

5. Pour into a 20cm/8in square baking tray and set aside to cool slightly then place in the fridge to chill completely.

6. Cut the fudge into squares with a sharp knife, turn out of the tin and store in an airtight container.

CHOKLADBOLLAR (THANKS TO BRISTOL HUNT SABOTEURS)

4 CUPS ROLLED OATS
1 1/4 CUPS BROWN SUGAR
1/2 CUP COCOA POWDER
1 CUP VEGAN BUTTER
1 TBSP ESPRESSO
1 TSP VANILLA EXTRACT
2 X 1 OZ SQUARES DARK CHOCOLATE
HALF CUP OF COCONUT FLAKES

Mix oats, sugar and cocoa powder together in a bowl.

Add the vegan butter and mix together until a thick dough is formed.

In a separate pan, mix the espresso, vanilla and dark chocolate. Stir together over a low heat until the chocolate is melted. Pour over the chocolate dough mixture and combine until thoroughly blended.

Pour coconut flakes into a bowl.

Roll small pieces of dough between your hands to make small balls about size of ping pong ball.

Roll the balls in the coconut, refrigerate for two hours, then eat.

CHERRY BAKEWELL CUPCAKES (THANKS TO EVOLVE! CAMPAIGNS

FOR THE CUPCAKE BASES:

2 AND A HALF CUPS PLAIN FLOUR
4 TSP BAKING POWDER
PINCH OF SALT
1 CUP SUGAR
1 CUP SOYA MILK OR ALMOND MILK
1/2 CUP SUNFLOWER OIL
2 TSP VANILLA ESSENCE
2 RIPE BANANAS, MASHED
1 TBSP APPLE CIDER VINEGAR
12 GLACE CHERRIES AND ICE CREAM SPRINKLES FOR DECORATION

1. Preheat the oven to 190 degrees.

2. Mix the milk, oil and essence together in a jug.

3. Sift the flour and baking powder into a mixing bowl. Add the sal
   and stir in the sugar.

4. Pour the wet ingredients from the jug into the dry, add the mashe
   bananas and mix together. Stir in the apple cider vinegar. The
   mixture will fluff up.

5. Spoon into cupcakes cases, filling two thirds of the way up. Bak
   the cakes for 15-20 minutes until the tops are springy and a
   cocktail stick inserted into the middle comes out clean. Let cool.

CHERRY BAKEWELL CUPCAKES (CONT'D)

FOR THE CHOCOLATE GANACHE:

1/2 CUP DARK CHOCOLATE CHIPS
1 TBSP DAIRY FREE MARGARINE (PURE OR VITALITE)
2 TBSP NON-DAIRY MILK (SOY, RICE, ALMOND, HAZELNUT, HEMP OR OAT)
1 TSP VANILLA ESSENCE

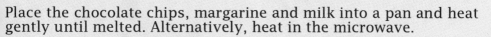

Place the chocolate chips, margarine and milk into a pan and heat gently until melted. Alternatively, heat in the microwave.

Allow to cool slightly and then stir in the vanilla essence.

FOR THE BUTTERCREAM ICING:

1/2 CUP DAIRY FREE MARGARINE (A HARD ONE LIKE STORK OR SOFT LIKE PURE OR VITALITE)
1/2 CUP VEGETABLE FAT (LIKE TREX)
4 CUPS ICING SUGAR
2-3 TABLESPOONS NON-DAIRY MILK (SOY, RICE, ALMOND, HAZELNUT, HEMP OR OAT)

In a food mixer, or with a hand held beater, cream the margarine and vegetable fat until it looks smooth and begins to fluff up a bit.

With the mixer on low speed, add the icing sugar bit by bit and mix for another few minutes until completely combined. Add enough of the milk to make the mixture fluffy and creamy but not too runny.

Pipe or spoon onto the cupcakes.

To decorate, drizzle with chocolate ganache, top with sprinkles and place a glace cherry on top of each cupcake.

CHOCOLATE COURGETTE CAKE

250G PLAIN FLOUR
350G CASTER SUGAR
85G COCOA POWDER
2 TEASPOONS BAKING POWDER
1 TEASPOON BICARBONATE OF SODA
300ML ALMOND MILK
125ML VEGETABLE OIL
2 TEASPOONS VANILLA EXTRACT TO TASTE
250G GRATED COURGETTES
75G DAIRY FREE SPREAD/VITALITE
4 1/2 TABLESPOONS BOILING WATER
375G ICING SUGAR
1 1/2 TABLESPOONS COCOA POWDER

1. Pre-heat the oven to 180°C or Gas 4.

2. Grease two 23cm (9 in) non-stick cake tins. Line the bottoms of the tins with parchment to stop the cake sticking.

3. In a large bowl, sieve together plain flour, caster sugar, cocoa baking powder and bicarbonate of soda.

4. Add almond milk, vanilla extract and vegetable oil. Mix well. Add grated courgettes and mix until all is well combined. Divide the mixture evenly between the two cake tins.

5. Bake for 25 to 30 minutes until an inserted cake skewer comes out clean. Leave the cakes to cool for 5 minutes in their tins then carefully pass a knife around the side of each cake tin to release it (or if you have them, use springform cake tins). Cool completely.

6. For the chocolate icing, melt the dairy-free spread with the boiling water in a bowl. In a separate bowl, mix together the icing sugar with sieved cocoa powder. Add the melted spread to the sugar mixture. Blend well until you have a smooth icing.

7. Layer up the cake with icing on top and in the middle, or add the jam of your choice in the centre.

MR B'S BISCUITS

60G GLUTEN FREE OATS
60G DESICCATED COCONUT
60G PLAIN, GLUTEN FREE FLOUR
60G LIGHT BROWN, SOFT SUGAR
2OZ VEGAN MARGARINE
1 1/2 TABLESPOONS GOLDEN SYRUP
1/4 LEVEL TEASPOON BICARBONATE OF SODA
1/2 TABLESPOON BOILING WATER
1/4 LEVEL TEASPOON GROUND GINGER (OPTIONAL)
40G PLAIN COOKING CHOCOLATE

Heat oven to 170°C (fan oven 150°C).

Melt the vegan margarine, syrup and sugar in a large saucepan.

Dissolve the bicarbonate of soda into the boiling water and mix in the remaining ingredients.

Place baking parchment on a baking tray, roll the mixture into walnut-sized balls, place far enough apart that they won't join as they bake and flatten them down gently before putting in the oven. Alternatively, you can do a very thin covering of the baking tray (just under 1cm thick) and cut into squares when baked.

Bake until golden – about 10 minutes on the top shelf.

Allow to cool or they'll fall apart as you dip them in the melted chocolate.

Place the chocolate in a pyrex mixing bowl and put it over a saucepan of water to melt the chocolate but don't let it boil.

Dip the cooled biscuits into the chocolate (between 1/3 and 1/2) and put them back onto the parchment for the chocolate to set.

To make flapjacks instead of biscuits, simply double the mixture and spread it 3cm thick on the baking parchment-covered baking tray. You can mix in sultanas, nuts etc. too but reduce the quantity of coconut to make space for them or they'll fall apart.

AQUAFABA MARSHMALLOW FLUFF MIX

THIS IS THE BASE FOR LOTS OF SWEET RECIPES. IT'S MADE WITH AQUAFABA (THE WATER FROM TINS OF CHICK PEAS). CREDIT TO SOOSE WALT AND THE "VEGAN MERINGUE HITS AND MISSES" GROUP ON FACEBOOK FOR THE DISCOVERY AND TESTING.

60ML AQUAFABA (CHICK PEA BRINE)
50G SUGAR
2TSP VANILLA ESSENCE
1/2 TSP CREAM OF TARTAR

Chill a tin of chickpeas in the fridge. When you're ready to star cooking, sieve the peas out for use in another recipe and retain th liquid in a large bowl. Using an electric mixer, start whisking. Ad the vanilla essence and the cream of tartar. Every few minutes, add one spoonful of the sugar. Keep whisking until soft peaks ar formed – this should be within ten minutes.

AMERICAN STYLE FLUFFY PANCAKES

FOR THE PANCAKES:
AQUAFABA MARSHMALLOW FLUFF MIX (AS ABOVE)
1/4 CUP OIL
2 TBS SUGAR
1 CUP PLANT BASED MILK
1 AND 1/4 CUP PLAIN FLOUR
2 TSP BAKING POWDER

FOR THE CHOCOLATE SAUCE:
CREAMED COCONUT
PLAIN DARK CHOCOLATE
WATER

1. In a different bowl, whisk together the sugar, oil and soy/nut mil with the vanilla essence.

2. Once an emulsified batter is formed, sift in the flour and bakin powder.

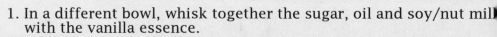

AMERICAN STYLE FLUFFY PANCAKES (CONT'D)

Fold the flour mix in very lightly with a spatula (this is not bread making, we want to maintain as much air in the mix as possible). Very gently fold in all of the aquafaba marshmallow fluff mix. You will be left with a very light and airy batter.

Heat a large non-stick frying pan to a gentle heat (expect the first pancake to be a test run to get the heat right).

Pour a dessert spoon-sized amount of batter onto the dry pan and manipulate it so that the mix spreads out evenly in a rough circular shape – it will start to rise and bubble quickly (the outside cooks much faster than the inside and they brown fast).

When the edges are bubbling, flip the pancake over and cook for another couple of minutes, then put aside ready to assemble the stack – make as many as you need.

Dissolve 1/3 pack of creamed coconut in enough warm water to make a sauce consistency. Once dissolved, add half a packet of chopped up dark vegan chocolate into the mix – keep it over enough heat to keep it loose and moving – usually chocolate will separate when used with water so make sure the coconut is dissolved properly first.

Pour over the warm pancakes and serve to your amazed guests. Put banana or other fruit between the layers, if desired.

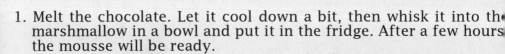

CHOCOLATE MOUSSE

AQUAFABA MARSHMALLOW FLUFF MIX (SEE PAGE 56)
1 BIG BAR OF DARK CHOCOLATE

1. Melt the chocolate. Let it cool down a bit, then whisk it into the marshmallow in a bowl and put it in the fridge. After a few hours the mousse will be ready.

2. Alternatively, you can freeze it to make chocolate ice cream.

SALTED CARAMEL AND PEANUT ICE CREAM

NOTE: IF YOU'RE MAKING AQUAFABA MARSHMALLOW FLUFF MIX JUST FOR THIS RECIPE THEN ONLY PUT IN HALF THE AMOUNT OF SUGAR BECAUSE THE CARAMEL WILL SWEETEN IT MORE.

1/2 CUP OF SUGAR
1 TBSP VEGAN MARGE
2 TBSP WATER
2 TBSP PEANUT FLOUR (YOU CAN GET IT IN FREE FROM SECTIONS OR HIPPY SHOPS)
2 TBSP SALTED PEANUTS

1. Melt the sugar in a pan on the hob to make a caramel. Keep an eye on it as it goes fast. As soon as it is liquid, take it off the heat and drop the marge in (careful, it spits). It'll probably go hard and lumpy, so put the water in and give it time to dissolve. It might need warming and stirring.

2. Chop up the peanuts small, then fold them and the flour into the aquafaba marshmallow fluff mix. It'll collapse a bit, but that's ok. Then do the same with the caramel. Freeze it.

Chocolate sauce that cracks when frozen is the perfect topping.